CLARINL
ONE HUNDRED
CLASSICAL
THEMES

Exclusive Distributors:
Music Sales Limited
8/9 Frith Street, London W1V 5TZ, England.
Music Sales Corporation
257 Park Avenue South, New York, NY10010. USA.
Music Sales Pty Limited
120 Rothschild Avenue, Rosebery, NSW 2018, Australia.

This book © Copyright 1991 by Wise Publications
Order No. AM84161
ISBN 0-7119-2588-7

Design by Hutton Staniford
Front cover photography by Stuart MacGregor

Music Sales' complete catalogue lists thousands of titles
and is free from your local music shop, or direct from
Music Sales Limited.
Please send a cheque/postal order for £1.50 for postage to:
Music Sales Limited, Newmarket Road, Bury St. Edmunds,
Suffolk IP33 3YB.

Your Guarantee of Quality
As publishers, we strive to produce every book to the
highest commercial standards.
The music has been freshly engraved and the book has
been carefully designed to minimise awkward page turns
and to make playing from it a real pleasure.
Particular care has been given to specifying acid-free,
neutral-sized paper which has not been elemental chlorine bleached
but produced with special regard for the environment.
Throughout, the printing and binding have been planned
to ensure a sturdy, attractive publication which should
give years of enjoyment.
If your copy fails to meet our high standards, please inform
us and we will gladly replace it.

Printed in the United Kingdom by
Caligraving Limited, Thetford, Norfolk.

Wise Publications
London/New York/Sydney

A MUSICAL JOKE

(K.522, 4th movement) Mozart

A POLICEMAN'S LOT IS NOT A HAPPY ONE

('The Pirates of Penzance') Sullivan

AIR ON THE G STRING

(Suite No.3, 2nd movement) Bach

AUTUMN

(The Four Seasons, No.3, 1st movement) Vivaldi

AUTUMN

(The Four Seasons, No.3, 3rd movement) Vivaldi

BARCAROLLE

('The Tales Of Hoffmann') Offenbach

BERCEUSE

(Dolly Suite Op.56) Fauré

Allegretto moderato

BOLERO

Ravel

Tempo di Bolero moderato assai ♩=72

BRIDAL MARCH

('Lohengrin') Wagner

Moderato con moto

BRIGG FAIR

(An English Rhapsody) Delius

BRINDISI

('La Traviata') Verdi

CHE FARÒ SENZA EURIDICE

('Orfeo ed Euridice') Gluck

Andante con moto

CLARINET CONCERTO

(K.622, 2nd movement) Mozart

Adagio

CLAIRE DE LUNE

(Suite Bergamasque) Debussy

Andante - très expressif

tempo rubato

peu à peu cresc. et animé

dim. molto

EINE KLEINE NACHTMUSIK

(K.525, 1st movement) Mozart

Allegro
8vb opt.

12

EMPEROR WALTZ

(op.437) Strauss

Tempo di valse

ESPANA

(Rhapsody for Orchestra) Chabrier

FARANDOLE

(L'Arlésienne Suite No.2) Bizet

FOR HE IS AN ENGLISHMAN

('HMS Pinafore') Sullivan

FÜR ELISE

Beethoven

GALOP INFERNAL

('Orpheus in the Underworld') Offenbach

GAUDEAMUS IGITUR

(Academic Festival Overture Op.80) Brahms

GAVOTTE

(Suite No.3, 3rd movement) Bach

[Allegro]

GOLLIWOGG'S CAKE WALK

(Children's Corner) Debussy

Allegro giusto

GYMNOPÉDIE NO.1

Satie

© Copyright 1991 Dorsey Brothers Limited, 8–9 Frith Street, London, W1V 5TZ.

Lent et douloureux

HABAÑERA

('Carmen') Bizet

Allegretto quasi andantino

HE SHALL FEED HIS FLOCK

('The Messiah') Handel

Larghetto e piano

HORN CONCERTO NO.4

(K.495, 3rd movement) Mozart

Allegro vivace

HORNPIPE

(The Water Music) Handel

Alla Hornpipe

HUMORESQUE

(Op.101 No.7) Dvořák

Poco lento e grazioso

HUNGARIAN DANCE NO.5

Brahms

JERUSALEM

Parry

JUPITER - I VOW TO THEE, MY COUNTRY

(The Planets Suite) Holst

LA CALINDA

('Koanga') Delius

Moderato, con grazia

p

LÀ CI DAREM LA MANO

('Don Giovanni') Mozart

Andante

mf

LA DONNA È MOBILE

('Rigoletto') Verdi

LAND OF HOPE AND GLORY

(Pomp & Circumstance March No.1 Op.39) Elgar

Allegro (largamente)

LARGO - OMBRA MAI FÙ

('Xerxes') Handel

Larghetto

LES SYLPHIDES

(Prelude Op.28 No.7) Chopin

Andantino

p dolce

dim.

pp

MARCH

(The Nutcracker Suite Op.71) Tchaikovsky

MINUET II

(Music for the Royal Fireworks) Handel

MORNING

(Peer Gynt Suite No.1 Op.46) Grieg

Allegretto pastorale

NIMROD

(Enigma Variations Op.36) Elgar

NOCTURNE

('A Midsummer Night's Dream' Op.61) Mendelssohn

Con moto tranquillo

NON PIÙ ANDRAI

('The Marriage of Figaro') Mozart

O FOR THE WINGS OF A DOVE

('Hear My Prayer') Mendelssohn

ODE TO JOY

(Symphony No.9 Op.125, 4th movement) Beethoven

ONE FINE DAY

('Madame Butterfly') Puccini

PAVANE

(Op.50) Fauré

Allegro moderato

PIANO CONCERTO

(Op.16, 1st movement) Grieg

Allegro molto moderato ♩=84

PIANO CONCERTO – 'ELVIRA MADIGAN'

(K.467, 2nd movement) Mozart

PIANO CONCERTO NO.1

(Op.23, 1st movement) Tchaikovsky

PIANO CONCERTO NO.3

(Op.37, 1st movement) Beethoven

Allegro con brio

PIANO CONCERTO NO.5 – 'THE EMPEROR'

(Op.73, 2nd movement) Beethoven

Adagio un poco mosso

POLOVTSIAN DANCES

('Prince Igor') Borodin

PIE JESU

(Requiem Op.48) Fauré

POMP & CIRCUMSTANCE MARCH NO.4

(Op.39) Elgar

POOR WAND'RING ONE

('The Pirates Of Penzance') Sullivan

39

PRELUDE

(L'Arlésienne Suite No.1) Bizet

Allegro deciso (tempo di marcia)

PRELUDE TO ACT III

('Lohengrin') Wagner

Molto vivace

PROMENADE

(Pictures At An Exhibition) Mussorgsky

Allegro giusto, nel modo russico; senza allegrezza, ma poco sostenuto

PRINCE IGOR OVERTURE

Borodin

Allegro

RADETSKY MARCH

(Op.228) Strauss

Allegro moderato

ROMEO AND JULIET

(Fantasy Overture) Tchaikovsky

Allegro giusto

RONDEAU

('Abdelazar') Purcell

ROSAMUNDE

(Entr'acte Act III) Schubert

44

SALUT D'AMOUR

(Op.12) Elgar

SERENADE

Schubert

SPARTACUS – 'THE ONEDIN LINE'

Khatchaturian

SPRING

(The Four Seasons, No.1, 1st movement) Vivaldi

ST ANTHONY CHORALE

(Variations on a Theme of Haydn Op.56a) Brahms

SWAN LAKE

(Op.20, Opening of Act II) Tchaikovsky

Moderato

SYMPHONIE FANTASTIQUE

(Op.14, 4th movement) Berlioz

Allegretto non troppo

SYMPHONY NO.1

(Op.68, 4th movement) Brahms

Allegro non troppo ma con brio

SYMPHONY NO.3

(Op.90, 3rd movement) Brahms

Poco allegretto

SYMPHONY NO.3 – 'THE EROICA'

(Op.55, 2nd movement)

Marcia funebre. Adagio assai. ♩=80

SYMPHONY NO.5

(Op.64, 2nd movement) Tchaikovsky

Andante cantabile, con alcuna licenza ♩.=54

SYMPHONY NO.6 – 'THE PASTORAL'

(Op.68, 5th movement) Beethoven

SYMPHONY NO.6 – 'THE PATHÉTIQUE'

(Op.74, 1st movement) Tchaikovsky

SYMPHONY NO.9 – 'THE GREAT'

(2nd movement) Schubert

Andante con moto

SYMPHONY NO.9 – 'NEW WORLD'

(Op.95, 2nd movement) Dvořák

Largo

SYMPHONY NO.9 – 'NEW WORLD'

(Op.95, 4th movement) Dvořák

Symphony No.94 – 'The Surprise'

(2nd movement) Haydn

TAKE A PAIR OF SPARKLING EYES

('The Gondoliers') Sullivan

Allegretto moderato

TANNHÄUSER OVERTURE

Wagner

Andante maestoso
tenuto molto

THE BLUE DANUBE

(Waltz, Op.314) Strauss

Tempo di valse

THE MERRY PEASANT

(Album for the Young Op.68 No.10) Schumann

THE TROUT PIANO QUINTET

(4th movement) Schubert

TOREADOR'S SONG

('Carmen') Bizet

TRISTESSE

(Étude Op.10 No.3) Chopin

TRUMPET VOLUNTARY

('The Prince of Denmark's March') Clarke

VALSE

('Coppélia') Delibes

VIOLIN CONCERTO

(Op.77, 2nd movement) Brahms

VIOLIN CONCERTO

(Op.61, 2nd movement) Elgar

VIOLIN CONCERTO

(Op.64, 2nd movement) Mendelssohn

WALTZ

('The Sleeping Beauty' Op.66) Tchaikovsky

Allegro (tempo di valse)

WEDDING MARCH

('A Midsummer Night's Dream' Op.61) Mendelssohn

WILLIAM TELL OVERTURE

Rossini

YOUR TINY HAND IS FROZEN

('La Bohème') Puccini

24th CAPRICE FOR SOLO VIOLIN

Paganini

10/96 (25932)